THE SECRET OF
ADORATION

THE SECRET OF
ADORATION

Andrew Murray

PUBLICATIONS

Fort Washington, PA 19034

The Secret of Adoration
Published by CLC Publications

U.S.A.
P.O. Box 1449, Fort Washington, PA 19034

UNITED KINGDOM
CLC International (UK)
Unit 5, Glendale Avenue, Sandycroft, Flintshire, CH5 2QP

Printed in the United States of America

ISBN (paperback): 978-1-61958-253-8
ISBN (e-book): 978-1-61958-254-5

Unless otherwise noted, all Scripture quotations are from the Holy Bible, New King James Version, copyright © 1979, 1980, 1982 by Thomas Nelson, Inc. Used by permission. All rights reserved.

Scripture quotations marked RV are from the Holy Bible, Revised Version, 1881.

Italics in Scripture quotations are the emphasis of the author.

Cover design by Mitch Bolton.

FOREWORD

WHEN *The Secret of Intercession* had been published in Dutch, it gave occasion to questions on the part of those who read it as to the greatness and the difficulty of the work. Many confessed that they knew little of such intercession as was spoken of and feared they would never attain to it.

They asked what might be the reason that among Christians there was so much reluctance to prayer.

A child finds it so natural and such a joy to be in the company of its father. What can it be that hinders God's children from taking full advantage of God's wonderful offer to receive them and to keep them in His Presence and, in answer to prayer, to bless them abundantly?

It was felt that one answer to the question as to the cause of the lack of power in prayer was this: we look too much to the human aspect and too little to the divine.

In prayer there are two parties: God and man. God in His inconceivable holiness and glory and love; man in his littleness, his sinfulness, his impotence. Our thought of what prayer is will depend on the point of view. If, as is mostly done, we just think of our own needs and desires, of our own efforts to pray and our own faith as to the certainty of an answer, we shall soon find that there is no real power in our prayer. It is only when we regard prayer in the light of God and the deep interest He takes in us, the wonderful love with which He waits to answer prayer, the almighty power which is the pledge of what He can and will do—and above all, the grace of our Lord Jesus Christ, and the Holy Spirit by which He Himself will strengthen us for the faith and perseverance that are needed—that we shall be able to know what joy and power there are in prayer. And we shall begin to see what an infinite difference it makes whether we look at prayer in the light of earth or of heaven, in the light of man's littleness or the infinite glory of the living God.

When once a Christian sees the difference, he may be in danger of at once striving to pray a little more and a little better than he has hitherto done and yet find how his efforts end in failure. He needs to realize that there are here two ways set before him. The one: prayer as a means by which man can get from Heaven what he needs. The other: prayer as an infinite grace of God, lifting us up into His fellowship and love, and then, when He has thus *brought us to Himself*, bestowing upon us the blessings we need. In the former case, the gifts that I can receive through prayer are the chief things. In the latter, God and His love, and intercourse with Him, and the surrender of the supplicant to His glory and His will, will be supreme. When once the child of God understands this, he sees that there is a great alternative set before him: Shall it be the human aspect of prayer or the divine that is to rule my life? Shall it be man or God that is to be first in every prayer? He will feel the need of coming to a definite decision as to which of these two paths he is to walk in. He will feel that it is no light matter to change from the one to the other. It is only possible by the intervention of God's mighty power, and by a surrender on one's own part in faith regarding what God will do, to begin walking with God as he has never yet done. Nothing but the firm resolve to part with the self-life in prayer and to yield himself wholly to the life and leading of the Spirit will enable him truly to become a man of prayer such as God and Christ would have him.

It was with the view of providing very simple help for all believers who are longing to enter into the wonderful privilege which is open to them through prayer that this second little book was written. It aims at reminding the reader day by day that in prayer, every day *God must be first*. To this end there must be secret prayer, where God and you alone can meet. The first thing must be to bow in lowly reverence before God in His glory—the Father whose name is to be hallowed—and so offer Him your adoration and worship. When you have secured some sense of His presence, you may utter your petitions in the hope, in the assurance, that He hears and accepts them, and in due time will send you His answer.

Above all, in our little book, we have felt a need for the unceasing repetition of this loving message: *take time*. Give God time to reveal Himself to you. Give yourself time to be silent and quiet before Him, waiting to receive through the Spirit the assurance of His presence with you, of His power working in you. Take time to read His Word, as in His presence, that from it you may know what He asks of you and what He promises you.

Let the Word create around you, create within you, a holy atmosphere, a holy heavenly light in which your soul will be refreshed and strengthened for the work of daily life. Yes, *take time* that God may let His holy presence enter into your heart; and in due time, your whole being may to some extent be permeated with the life and the love of Heaven.

It was under the influence of thoughts and prayers such as these that this little book was written in its Dutch form. There are evidences of its having been a help to many. One minister wrote that he had just read it twice and intended going through it a third time and giving each of his children a copy.

I feel deeply the need of Christians being trained to pray, if their intercession is to be effectual and much availing. It may be that it will please God to grant some of His children, who, in Bible classes or otherwise, are seeking to make those around them sharers in the blessings they enjoy, to use it as a help to bring young or feeble Christians deeper into that blessed life of joy and power which is waiting for them. They only need to learn how to live their life with God aright in the daily exercise of fellowship with Him through the prayer of faith. They will then find that the path of prayer in which it is always *God first* is not only the path of great peace and joy, but of true power for intercession on behalf of those who have yet to be won for Him. It is my humble prayer that God may graciously bless the booklet to many of His children.

ANDREW MURRAY

God reveals His presence:
Let us now adore Him,
And with awe appear before Him.
God is in His temple:
All within keep silence,
Prostrate lie with deepest reverence.
Him alone, God we own,
Him our God and Saviour,
Praise His name for ever.
"Worship God."—Rev. 22:9

True Worship

"Worship God."

THOSE who have read the booklet *The Secret of Intercession* have doubtless more than once asked, "Why are prayer and intercession not a greater joy and delight? Is there any way that we may be able to make fellowship with God our chief joy and, as intercessors, bring down His power and blessing on those for whom we pray?"

There may be more than one answer to the question, but the main one is undoubtedly that we know God too little. In our prayer, we do not seek His presence; it is not the main thing on which we set our hearts. And yet it should be so. We think mostly of ourselves, our need, our weakness, our desire and prayer.

We forget that in every prayer *God must be First, must be All.* To seek Him, to find Him, to wait in His presence, to be assured that *His holy presence rests upon us,* that He actually listens to what we say and is working in us—this alone is what makes prayer as natural and easy to us as the loving fellowship of a child with his father.

How is one to attain to this nearness to God and fellowship with Him? The answer is simple: *We must give God time to make Himself known to us.* Believe with your whole heart that just as you present yourself to God as a petitioner, so God presents Himself to you as the Hearer of prayer. But you cannot realize this until you give Him time and quiet. It is not the quantity or earnestness of your words that give prayer its power, but the living faith that *God Himself is taking you and your prayer into His loving heart.* He Himself will give the assurance that in His time your prayer will be heard.

Begin this day with the words, "To you, O LORD, I lift up my soul" (Ps. 25:1). Bow before Him in stillness, believing that He looks on you and will reveal His presence.

"My soul thirsts for God, for the living God" (42:2).

God Is a Spirit

"God is Spirit, and those who worship Him must worship in spirit and truth."

John 4:24

WHEN God created man and breathed into him of His own spirit, man became a living soul. The soul stood midway between the spirit and the body, and had to yield either to the spirit, to be lifted up to God, or yield to the flesh and its lusts. In the Fall, man refused to listen to the spirit and became the slave of the body. The spirit in man became utterly darkened.

In regeneration the spirit is quickened and born again from above. In the regenerate life of fellowship with God, the spirit of man always has to yield itself to the Spirit of God. The spirit is the deepest, most inward part of the human being. We read in Psalm 51:6, "You desire truth in the inward parts, and in the hidden part You will make me to know wisdom"; and in Jeremiah 31:33, "I will put My law in their minds, and write it on their hearts." Isaiah also says, "With my soul I have desired You in the night, yes, by my spirit within me I will seek You early" (26:9). The soul must sink down into the depths of the hidden spirit and call upon that to stir itself to seek God.

God is a Spirit, most holy and most glorious. He gave us a spirit so that we could have fellowship with Him. Through sin that power was darkened and nearly quenched. The only way to restore it is by presenting the soul in stillness before God to let His Holy Spirit work in our spirit. Deeper than our thoughts and feelings, God will in our inward part—in the spirit within us, if it has been regenerated—teach us to worship Him in spirit and in truth.

"The Father is seeking such to worship Him" (John 4:23). His Holy Spirit will teach us this if we wait on Him. Be still before God and yield your whole heart to believe in and to receive the gentle working of His Spirit. And breathe out such words as these: "My soul, be silent before God"; "With my soul I have desired You in the night, yes, by my spirit within me I will seek You early" (Isa. 26:9); "On You, O God, I wait."

Intercession and Adoration

Oh, worship the Lord in the beauty of holiness!
Psalm 96:9

THE better we know God the more wonderful becomes our insight into the power of intercession. We begin to understand that it is the great means by which man can take part in carrying out God's purpose. God has entrusted the whole of His redemption in Christ to His *people*—to make it known and to communicate its loveliness to men. In all this, intercession is the chief and essential element; it is how His servants enter into full fellowship with Christ and receive the power of the Spirit for service.

It is easy to see why God has so ordered it. God desires to renew us after His image and likeness, and the only way to do this is by making His desires our own, so that we breathe His disposition and in love sacrifice ourselves. Then we become, in a measure, like Christ, who "always lives to make intercession" (Heb. 7:25). Such can be the life of the consecrated believer.

The clearer our insight into this great purpose of God, the more we will feel the need to enter into God's presence in a spirit of humble worship and holy adoration. When we take time to abide in God's presence and enter fully into His mind and will, our whole soul becomes possessed by the thought of His glorious purpose. This strengthens our faith that God will work out all the good pleasure of His will through our prayers. As the glory of God shines upon us and we realize how helpless we are, we rise to a level of faith that believes that God will do above all that we can ask or think (see Eph. 3:20). Intercession leads us to see our need for deeper adoration, and adoration gives us new power for intercession. The two will be found to be inseparable.

The secret of true adoration can only be known by the soul that takes time to wait in God's presence—the soul that yields itself to God for Him to reveal Himself. Adoration prepares us for the great work of making God's glory known. "Oh come, let us worship and bow down; let us kneel before the LORD our Maker. For He is our God. . . . Give to the LORD the glory due His name" (Ps. 95:6–7; 96:8).

The Desire For God

With my soul I have desired You in the night.

Isaiah 26:9

WHAT is the greatest and most glorious thing that man can find upon earth? It is nothing less than God Himself.

And what is the best and most glorious thing that a man needs to do every day? It is nothing less than to seek and know and love and praise this glorious God. As glorious as God is, so is the glory which begins to work in the heart and life of those who give themselves to God.

Have you learned this first and greatest thing you need to do every day—to seek this God, to meet Him, worship Him, live for Him and for His glory? It is a great step forward in the life of a Christian when he truly sees this and yields himself to consider fellowship with God every day as the chief end of his life.

Take time to ask yourself if this is not the truest, highest wisdom and the one purpose for which a Christian is above all to live—to know his God rightly, and to love Him with his whole heart. It is not only true, but God Himself strongly desires that you live this way with Him and, in answer to prayer, will enable you to do so.

Begin today. Take a word from God's Book to speak to Him in stillness of soul: "O God, You are my God; early will I seek You; my soul thirsts for You; my flesh longs for You . . . my soul follows close behind You.

. . . With my whole heart I have sought You" (Ps. 63:1, 8; 119:10).

Repeat these words in deep reverence and childlike longing till their spirit and power enter your heart; and wait upon God till you begin to realize the blessedness of meeting with Him. As you persevere, you will learn to expect that holy fear and sense of God's presence to abide with you throughout the day.

"I waited patiently for the LORD; and He inclined to me, and heard my cry" (40:1).

Silent Adoration

Truly my soul silently waits for God . . . My soul, wait
silently for God alone, for my expectation is from Him.
Psalm 62:1, 5

WHEN man in his littleness and God in His glory meet, we all understand that what God says has infinitely more worth than what man says. And yet our prayers so often consist of our thoughts, of what we need, that we give God no time to speak to us. Our prayers are often so indefinite and vague. It is a great lesson to learn that to be silent before God is the secret of true adoration. Remember these promises: "In quietness and confidence shall be your strength" (Isa. 30:15); "I wait for the LORD, my soul waits, and in His word I do hope" (Ps. 130:5).

As the soul bows itself before Him, remembering His greatness, holiness, power and love, and seeking to give Him the honor, reverence and worship due Him, the heart will be open to sense the nearness of God and the working of His power.

Such worship of God—in which you bow low in your nothingness, and realize God's presence as He gives Himself to you in Christ Jesus—is the sure way to give Him the glory due Him; it leads to the highest blessedness to be found in prayer.

Do not imagine that it is time lost. Do not turn from it if at first it seems difficult or fruitless. Be assured that it brings you into a right relation to God. It opens the way to fellowship with Him. It leads to the blessed assurance that He is looking on you in tender love and working in you with a secret, divine power. As you become more accustomed to it, it will give you the sense of His presence abiding with you throughout the day. It will make you strong to testify for God. Someone has said, "No one is able to influence others for goodness and holiness beyond the amount that there is of God in him." People will begin to feel that you have been with God.

"The LORD is in His holy temple. Let all the earth keep silence before Him" (Hab. 2:20). "Be silent, all flesh, before the LORD, for He is aroused from His holy habitation!" (Zech. 2:13).

The Light of God's Countenance

God is light.

1 John 1:5

The Lord is my light.

Psalm 27:1

EVERY morning the sun rises, and we walk in its light and perform our daily duties with gladness. Whether we think of it or not, the light of the sun shines on us all day.

Every morning the light of God shines on His children. But in order to enjoy the light of God's countenance, the soul must turn to God and trust Him to let His light shine in on it.

When there is a shipwreck at midnight, the sailors long for morning. How often the sigh goes up, "When will the day break?" In the same way, the Christian must wait on God patiently until His light shines on him. "My soul waits for the LORD more than those who watch for the morning" (130:6).

Begin each day with one of these prayers: "Make Your face shine upon Your servant" (31:16); "LORD, lift up the light of Your countenance upon us" (4:6); "Cause Your face to shine, and we shall be saved!" (80:3).

Do not rest until you know that the light of His countenance and His blessing is resting on you. Then you will experience the truth of the Scripture, "They walk, O

LORD, in the light of Your countenance. In Your name they rejoice all day long" (Ps. 89:15–16).

The ardent longing of your Father is that you may dwell and rejoice in His light all day. Just as you need the light of the sun each hour, so the heavenly light, the light of the countenance of the Father, is indispensable. Just as we receive and enjoy the light of the sun, we can be confident that God desires to let His light shine on us.

Even when there are clouds, we still have the sun. Even in the midst of difficulties the light of God will rest on you without ceasing. If you are sure that the sun has risen, you count upon its light all the day. Make sure that the light of God shines upon you in the morning and you can count upon that light being with you all day long.

Do not rest until you have said, "Lord, lift up the light of Your countenance upon us." Take time till that light shines in your heart, and you can truly say, "The LORD is my light and my salvation" (27:1).

Faith In God

[Jesus] said to them, "Have faith in God."

Mark 11:22

J UST as the eye is the organ by which we see light, so faith is the power by which we see the light of God and walk in it.

Man was made for God—made in His likeness; his whole being was formed after the divine pattern. Think of mankind's wonderful power of thinking out the thoughts of God hidden in nature. Think of the human heart, with its unlimited powers of self-sacrifice and love. Man was made for God, to seek Him, to find Him, to grow into His likeness and show forth His glory—in the fullest sense, to be His dwelling. And faith is the eye which, turning away from the world and self, looks up to God and in His light sees light. To faith God reveals Himself.

How often we try to awaken thoughts and feelings toward God which are but a faint shadow, and we forget to gaze on the Incomparable Original. Could we but realize it, in the depth of our soul *God reveals Himself*!

Without faith it is impossible to please God or to know Him. In our quiet time we have to pray to our Father who is in the secret place. There He hides us in the secret place (see Ps. 27:5). And there, as we wait and worship before Him, He will—just as the light by its very nature reveals itself—let His light shine into our heart. May our one desire be to take time and be still before

God, believing with an unbounded faith in His longing to make Himself known to us. May we feed on God's Word, making us strong in faith. May that faith have large thoughts of God's glory, of His power to reveal Himself to us, of His longing to get complete possession of us.

Such faith, exercised and strengthened day by day in secret fellowship with God, will become the habit of our life, keeping us ever in the enjoyment of His presence and the experience of His saving power.

"[Abraham] was strengthened in faith, giving glory to God, being fully convinced that what He had promised He was also able to perform" (Rom. 4:20–21).

"I believe God that it will be just as it was told me" (Acts 27:25).

"Wait on the LORD; be of good courage, and He shall strengthen your heart; wait, I say, on the LORD!" (Ps. 27:14).

Alone With God

And it happened, as He was alone praying.
Luke 9:18

He departed again to a mountain by Himself alone.
John 6:15

MAN needs God. God made him for Himself, to find his life and happiness in Him alone. Man needs to be alone with God. His fall consisted of his being brought under the power of things visible and temporal through the lust of the flesh and the world. His restoration is meant to bring him back to the Father's house, to His presence, to His love and fellowship. Salvation means being brought to love and delight in the presence of God.

Man needs to be alone with God. Without this, God cannot have the opportunity to shine into his heart and transform his nature, to take possession of him and fill him with the fullness of God.

Man needs to be alone with God in order to yield himself to the presence and the power of His holiness and love. Christ could not live here on earth without at times separating Himself entirely from His surroundings and being alone with God. How much more must this be indispensable to us! When our Lord commanded us to enter our inner chamber, shut the door, and pray to our Father in secret, He promised us that the Father would hear such prayers and mightily answer them. Alone with God—that is the secret of true prayer, of true power in prayer; of authentic, face-to-face fellowship with God, of power for service. There is no true, deep conversion, no real holiness, no clothing with the Holy Spirit and power, no abiding peace or joy, without a daily time alone with God. There is no path to holiness other than frequent and lengthy times alone with God.

What a privilege it is to begin every morning in daily secret prayer. May it be the one thing our hearts are set on.

Take time to be alone with God. Soon it will amaze you to hear someone suggest that five minutes could be enough. "Give heed to the voice of my cry, my King and my God, for to You I will pray. My voice You shall hear in the morning, O Lord; in the morning I will direct it to You, and I will look up" (Ps. 5:2–3).

Wholly For God

Whom have I in heaven but You? And there is none upon earth that I desire besides You.

Psalm 73:25

ALONE with God—this is a word of the deepest importance. May we seek grace from God to reach its depths. Then we will learn another word of equally deep significance: wholly for God. If we find that it is not easy to persevere in being alone with God we will realize that it is because we are not wholly for God.

Because He is the only God, He alone has a right to demand that we be wholly for Him. Without this surrender He cannot make His power known. We read in the Old Testament that His servants Abraham, Moses, Elijah and David gave themselves wholly and unreservedly to God so that He could work out His plans through them. It is only the fully surrendered heart that can fully trust God for all He has promised.

If anyone desires to do a great work he must give himself wholly to it. This is especially true of a mother's care for her child. She gives herself wholly to the little one whom she loves. Is it not reasonable that the great God of Love should have us wholly for Himself? "Wholly for God" should be the keynote for our devotions every morning as we rise. As wholly as God gives Himself to us, so He desires that we give ourselves to Him. Meditate on these things alone with God and ask Him by

His almighty power to work in you all that is pleasing in His sight. Wholly for God—what a privilege! What wonderful grace to fit us for it! Wholly for God means separation from men, and work, and all that might draw us away. Wholly for God leads to indescribable blessedness as the soul learns what it means and what God gives with it. "You shall love the LORD your God with all your heart, with all your soul, and with all your mind" (Matt. 22:37). "They . . . sought Him with all their soul; and He was found by them" (2 Chron. 15:15). "With my whole heart I have sought You" (Ps. 119:10).

The Knowledge of God

"And this is eternal life, that they may know You."
John 17:3

THE knowledge of God is absolutely necessary for the spiritual life; it is *life eternal*. I don't mean the intellectual knowledge we receive from others, but the living, experiential knowledge in which God makes Himself known to the soul. Just as the rays of the sun on a cold winter's day warm the body, so the living God sheds the life-giving rays of His holiness and love into the heart that waits on Him.

Why do we so seldom experience this life-giving power of the true knowledge of God? It is because we do not give God time to reveal Himself to us. When we pray, we think we know how to speak to God, but we forget that one of the first steps in prayer is to be silent before God, that He may reveal Himself. By His hidden but mighty power, God manifests His presence, resting on us and working in us. To know God in the personal experience of His presence is life indeed.

Brother Lawrence had a great longing to know God and for this purpose went into a monastery. His spiritual advisers gave him prayer books to use, but he put them aside. "It helps little to pray," he said, "if I do not know the God to whom I pray." He believed that God would reveal Himself. He remained a long time in silent adoration in order to become fully aware of the presence of this great and holy Being. He continued in this practice, until the day came when he lived consciously and constantly in God's presence, experiencing His blessed nearness and keeping power.

As the rising sun gives the promise of light throughout the day, so a quiet time of waiting on God, yielding ourselves to let Him shine on us, gives the promise of His presence and power resting on us all day. Be sure that the sun has risen on your soul.

As the sun on a cold day shines on us and imparts its warmth, the living God will work in us with His love and almighty power. God will reveal Himself as life and light and joy and strength to the soul that waits upon Him. "Lord, lift up the light of Your countenance upon us" (Ps. 4:6). "Be still, and know that I am God" (46:10).

God the Father

*"Make disciples . . . baptizing them in the name of the
Father and of the Son and of the Holy Spirit."*

Matthew 28:19

THE doctrine of the Holy Trinity has a deep devotional aspect. As we think of God the Father we remember the inconceivable distance that separates Him in His holiness from sinful men, and we bow in deep contrition and holy fear. As we think of Christ the Son we remember the inconceivable nearness in which He came to be born of a woman, to die an accursed death, and so be inseparably joined to us for all eternity. And as we think of the Holy Spirit we remember the inconceivable blessedness of God having His abode in us and making us His home and His temple through eternity.

When Christ taught us to say, "Our Father in heaven," He immediately added, "hallowed be Your name" (6:9). As God is holy, so we are to be holy too. And there is no way of becoming holy but by counting that name most holy and drawing near to Him in prayer.

How often we speak that name—Father—without any sense of the unspeakable privilege of our relation to God. If we would just take time to come into contact with God and to worship Him in His Father love, the inner chamber of our hearts would become to us the gate of heaven! If you pray to your Father in secret, bow very low before Him and seek to adore His name as most holy. Remember that this is the highest blessedness of prayer. "Pray to your Father who is in the secret place; and your Father who sees in secret will reward you openly" (Matt. 6:6).

What an unspeakable privilege, to be alone with God in secret and say, "My Father"—to have the assurance that He has indeed seen me in that secret place and will reward me openly. Take time in private prayer until you can say with Jacob, "I have seen God face to face, and my life is preserved" (Gen. 32:30).

God the Son

Grace to you and peace from God our Father and the Lord Jesus Christ.

Romans 1:7

IT is remarkable that the Apostle Paul in each of his thirteen Epistles writes (with only minor variances), "Grace to you and peace from God our Father and the Lord Jesus Christ." He had such a deep sense of the inseparable oneness of the Father and the Son in the work of grace that in each opening benediction he refers to both.

This is a lesson for us of the utmost importance. There may be times in our Christian life when we think mostly of God the Father, and pray to Him. But later on we realize that it may cause spiritual loss if we do not grasp the truth that only through faith in Christ and in living union with Him can we enjoy a full and abiding fellowship with God.

In Revelation, John saw "a throne set in heaven, and One sat on the throne. . . . The four living creatures . . . do not rest day or night, saying: 'Holy, holy, holy, Lord God Almighty, who was and is and is to come!'" (Rev. 4:2, 8).

Later he saw "in the midst of the throne . . . a Lamb as though it had been slain" (5:6). No one in all the worshiping multitude could see God unless he first saw Christ the Lamb of God. And no one could see Christ without seeing the glory of God the Father and Son as inseparably One.

If you want to know and worship God rightly, seek Him and worship Him in Christ. And if you seek Christ, seek Him and worship Him in God. Then you will understand what it is to have your life "hidden with Christ in God" (Col. 3:3). Then you will experience the fellowship and adoration of Christ that is indispensable to the full knowledge of the love and holiness of God.

Be still, and speak these words in deepest reverence: "Grace and peace"—all I can desire—"from God our Father and the Lord Jesus Christ."

Take time to meditate, and then believe and expect all from God the Father who sits on the throne and from the Lord Jesus Christ, the Lamb in the midst of the throne. Then you will learn truly to worship God. Return frequently to this sacred scene, to give "glory . . . to Him who sits on the throne, and to the Lamb" (Rev. 5:13).

God the Holy Spirit

Through Him we both have access by one Spirit to the Father.
Ephesians 2:18

IN our communion with God in the inner chamber of our hearts, we must guard against the danger of seeking to know God and Christ in the power of the intellect or the emotions. The Holy Spirit has been given for the express purpose that we may have access to the Father through the Son (see 2:18). Let us be careful to wait for the teaching of the Spirit so that our labor is not in vain.

Christ taught His disciples this truth after their meal on the last night. Speaking of the soon coming of the Holy Spirit, He said, "Until now you have asked nothing in My name. Ask, and you will receive, that your joy may be full" (John 16:24). The Holy Spirit was given with the one great objective of teaching us to pray. He makes our fellowship with the Father and the Son a blessed reality. Be strong in faith that He is working secretly in you. As you enter the inner chamber, give yourself wholly to His guidance as your Teacher in all your intercession and adoration.

When Christ said to the disciples on the evening of the resurrection day, "Receive the Holy Spirit" (20:22), it was, for one thing, to strengthen and prepare them for the ten days of prayer that followed His ascension, and for their receiving the fullness of the Spirit. This suggests to us three things we ought to remember when we draw near to God in prayer:

1. We must pray in confidence that the Holy Spirit dwells in us, and yield ourselves, in stillness of soul, definitely to His leading. Take time for this.

2. We must believe that the "greater works" of the Spirit for the enlightening and strengthening of the spiritual life—the fullness of the Spirit—will be given in answer to prayer.

3. We must believe that through the Spirit, in unity with all God's children, we may ask for and expect the mighty workings of that Spirit on His church and people.

"He who believes in Me, as the Scripture has said, out of his heart will flow rivers of living water" (John 7:38). Do you believe this?

The Secret of the Lord

"Go into your room, and when you have shut your door, pray to your Father who is in the secret place; and your Father who sees in secret will reward you openly."

Matthew 6:6

CHRIST greatly longed for His disciples to know God as their Father and have secret fellowship with Him. In His own life He found it not only indispensable but the highest happiness to meet the Father in secret. And He wants us to realize that it is impossible to be true, wholehearted disciples without daily communion with the Father in heaven, who waits for us in the secret place of prayer.

God is a God who hides Himself from the world and all that is of the world. God wants to draw us away from the world and from ourselves. He offers us instead the blessedness of close, intimate communion with Himself. Oh, that God's children would understand this!

Believers in the Old Testament enjoyed this experience: "You are my hiding place" (Ps. 32:7); "He who dwells in the secret place of the Most High shall abide under the shadow of the Almighty" (91:1); "The secret of the LORD is with those who fear Him" (25:14).

Christians in the New Covenant ought to value this secret communion with God all the more. Paul tells us, "You died, and your life is hidden with Christ in God" (Col. 3:3). If we really believe this, we will have the joyful assurance that our life, hidden with Christ in God in such divine keeping, is safe and beyond the reach of every foe. We should confidently seek the renewal of our spiritual life through daily prayer to our Father who is in the secret place. Because we are dead with Christ, planted with Him in the likeness of His death and resurrection, we know that, as the roots of a tree are hidden under the earth, so the roots of our daily life are hidden deep in God.

Take the time to realize that God will hide you in the secret place of His presence (see Ps. 31:20). Your first thought in prayer should be that you are alone with God, and that God is with you. "In the secret place of His tabernacle He shall hide me" (27:5).

Half an Hour Silence in Heaven

*There was silence in heaven for about half an hour. . . . Then
another angel, having a golden censer, came and stood at
the altar. He was given much incense, that he should offer it
with the prayers of all the saints upon the golden altar
which was before the throne.*

Revelation 8:1, 3

THERE was silence in heaven for about half an
hour to bring the prayers of the saints before God,
before the first angel sounded his trumpet. And so ten
thousands of God's children have felt the absolute need
of silence and retirement from the things of earth for half
an hour—to present their prayers before God and in fellowship with Him be strengthened for their daily work.

How often the complaint is heard that there is no
time for prayer. And often the confession is made that,
even if time could be found, one feels unable to spend
it in real communion with God. We need not ask what
prevents us from growing in our spiritual lives. The secret of strength can only be found in living communion
with God.

Just obey Christ when He says, "When you have
shut your door, pray to your Father who is in the secret
place" (Matt. 6:6), and have the courage to be alone with
God for half an hour. Do not worry that you won't know
how to spend the time. Just begin and be faithful, and
bow in silence before God, and He will reveal Himself
to you. If you need help, read a passage of Scripture,

and let God's Word speak to you. Then bow in deepest humility before God, and wait on Him. *He will work within you*. Read Psalm 61, 62 or 63, and speak the words out before God. Then begin to pray. Intercede for your own household and children, for the congregation and minister, for schools and missions. Keep on, though the time may seem long. God will reward you. But above all, be sure you meet God.

God longs to bless you. Isn't it worth the trouble to take half an hour alone with God? In heaven itself there was need for half an hour's silence to present the prayers of the saints before God. If you persevere, you may find that the half-hour that seems the most difficult in the whole day may eventually become the most blessed in your whole life. "Truly my soul silently waits for God. . . . My soul, wait silently for God alone, for my expectation is from Him" (Ps. 62:1, 5).

God's Greatness

For you are great, and do wondrous things; You alone are God.

Psalm 86:10

WHEN anyone begins an important work, he takes time to consider the greatness of his undertaking. Astronomers spend years of labor to grasp the magnitude of the heavenly bodies. Isn't our glorious God worthy of any time we take to know and adore His greatness?

Yet how superficial is our knowledge of God's greatness. We do not allow ourselves time to bow before Him and come under the deep impression of His incomprehensible majesty and glory. Meditate on the following texts until you are filled with some sense of what a glorious Being God is: "Great is the Lord, and greatly to be praised; and His greatness is unsearchable. . . . I will declare Your greatness. . . . They shall utter the memory of Your great goodness" (145:3, 6, 7).

Do not imagine that it is easy to grasp the meaning of these words. Take time for them to master your heart, until you bow in speechless adoration before God. This is what Jeremiah did: "Ah, Lord God! . . . There is nothing too hard for You. . . . the Great, the Mighty God . . . great in counsel and mighty in work" (Jer. 32:17–19). And hear God's answer: "Behold, I am the LORD, the God of all flesh. Is there anything too hard for Me?" (32:27). The right comprehension of God's greatness will take time. But if we give God the honor that is His due, and if our faith grows strong in the knowledge of what a great and powerful God we have, we will be motivated to spend time in the inner chamber of our hearts and bow in humble worship before this great and mighty God. In His abundant mercy He will teach us through the Holy Spirit to say, "The LORD is the great God, and the great King above all gods. . . . Oh come, let us worship and bow down; let us kneel before the LORD our Maker" (Ps. 95:3, 6).

A Perfect Heart

For the eyes of the LORD run to and fro throughout the whole earth, to show Himself strong on behalf of those whose heart is loyal to [perfect toward, KJV] Him.

2 Chronicles 16:9

IN worldly matters we know how important it is that work should be done with the whole heart. In the spiritual sphere this is likewise true. God has given the commandment, "You shall love the LORD your God with all your heart, with all your soul, and with all your strength" (Deut. 6:5). And in Jeremiah 29:13 it says, "You will seek Me and find Me, when you search for Me with all your heart."

It is amazing that earnest Christians who tackle their daily work with all their hearts are so content to take things easy in the service of God. They do not seem to realize that, if anywhere, they should give themselves to God's service with all the power of their will.

The text above gives us an insight into the absolute necessity of seeking God with a perfect or loyal heart. What an encouragement this should be to us to humbly wait upon God with an upright heart; we can be assured that His eye is upon us, and He will show forth His mighty power in us and in our work.

Have you learned this lesson in your worship of God—to yield yourself each morning with your whole heart to do God's will? Pray each prayer with a perfect heart, in true wholehearted devotion to Him, and in faith expect the power of God to work in you and through you. Remember that to come to this you must begin by being silent before God, until you realize that He is indeed working in the secret place of your heart. "I wait for my God" (Ps. 69:3). "In the secret place of His tabernacle He shall hide me" (27:5).

The Omnipotence of God

"I am Almighty God."

Genesis 17:1

WHEN Abraham heard these words, he fell on his face, and God spoke to him, filling his heart with faith in what God would do for him. Have you bowed in deep humility before God until you sensed your living contact with the Almighty, until your heart was filled with faith that the mighty God is working in you and will perfect His work in you?

Read how the psalmists rejoiced in God and in His strength: "I will love You, O LORD, my strength" (Ps. 18:1); "The LORD is the strength of my life" (27:1); "God is the strength of my heart" (73:26); "You . . . made me bold with strength in my soul" (138:3). Also look at such passages as Psalm 18:32, 46:1, 68:28, 68:35, 59:17 and 89:17. Take time to appropriate these words, and to adore God as the Almighty One, your strength.

Christ taught us that salvation is the work of God and quite impossible for man. When the disciples asked, "Who then can be saved?" His answer was, "With men this is impossible, but with God all things are possible" (Matt. 19:25, 26). If we firmly believe this, we will also believe that God is working in us all that is pleasing in His sight.

Paul prayed for the Ephesians that through the enlightening of the Spirit they might know "the exceeding greatness of His power toward us who believe, according to the working of His mighty power" (Eph. 1:19). And he prayed for the Colossians that they would be "strengthened with all might, according to His glorious power" (1:11). When we fully believe that the mighty power of God is working without ceasing within us, we can joyfully say, "God is the strength of my life."

Is it any wonder that many Christians complain of weakness and shortcomings? They do not understand that the Almighty God must work in them every hour of the day. That is the secret of the true life of faith. Do not rest until you can say to God, "I will love You, O Lord, my strength." Let God have complete possession of you and you will be able to say with all God's people, "You are the glory of their strength" (Ps. 89:17).

The Fear of God

Blessed is the man who fears the LORD, who delights greatly in His commandments.

Psalm 112:1

THE fear of God—these words characterize the religion of the Old Testament and the foundation which it laid for the more abundant life of the New. The gift of holy fear is still the great desire of the child of God, and needs to be an essential part of any life that is to make a real impression on the world around it. It is one of the great promises of the new covenant in Jeremiah: "I will make an everlasting covenant with them . . . I will put My fear in their hearts so that they will not depart from Me" (32:40).

We find the perfect combination of two seeming opposites—fear and comfort—in Acts 9:31: "Then the churches . . . had peace and were edified. And walking in the fear of the Lord and in the comfort of the Holy Spirit, they were multiplied." Paul more than once gives fear a high place in the Christian life: "Work out your own salvation with fear and trembling; for it is God who works in you" (Phil. 2:12–13); ". . . perfecting holiness in the fear of God" (2 Cor. 7:1).

It has often been said that one of the ways in which our modern era does not compare favorably with the times of the Puritans and the Covenanters is our lack of the fear of God. No wonder, then, that there is a corresponding lack of the reading of God's Word, regular worshiping in His house, and the spirit of continuous prayer—all of which marked the early church. It is essential that we preach on Scripture passages like those above and teach young believers about the need and the blessedness of a deep fear of God; this will lead to unceasing prayerfulness—one of the essential elements of the life of faith.

We must earnestly cultivate this grace in the inner chamber of our hearts, until we hear this word from heaven: "Who shall not fear You, O Lord, and glorify Your name? For You alone are holy" (Rev. 15:4). "Let us have grace, by which we may serve God acceptably with reverence and godly fear" (Heb. 12:28).

When we take the promise "Blessed is the man who fears the LORD" (Ps. 112:1) into our hearts and believe that it is one of the deepest secrets of blessedness, we will truly seek, every time we approach God, to worship Him in reverential fear. "Serve the LORD with fear, and rejoice with trembling" (2:11).

God Incomprehensible

"Behold, God is great, and we do not know Him. . . . As for
the Almighty, we cannot find Him; He is excellent in power."
Job 36:26; 37:23

THIS attribute of God as a Spirit whose being and glory are entirely beyond our power of apprehension is one that we ponder all too little. And yet in the spiritual life it is of utmost importance to be deeply aware that, as the heavens are high above the earth, so God's thoughts and ways are infinitely exalted beyond ours.

We must look to God with deep humility and holy reverence, and then with childlike simplicity, yield ourselves to the teaching of His Holy Spirit. "Oh, the depth of the riches both of the wisdom and knowledge of God! How unsearchable are His judgments and His ways past finding out!" (Rom. 11:33).

Let us respond in our hearts, "O Lord, how wonderful are all Your thoughts, and how deep are Your purposes." The study of God's attributes should fill us with holy awe and a sacred longing to know Him and honor Him properly.

Just think of His greatness—incomprehensible; His might—incomprehensible; His omnipresence—incomprehensible; His wisdom—incomprehensible; His holiness—incomprehensible; His mercy—incomprehensible; His love—incomprehensible. As you worship, cry out, "What an inconceivable glory is in this Great Being who is my God and Father!" Then confess with shame how little you have sought to know Him properly, or to wait on Him to reveal Himself. Begin in faith to trust that, in a way passing all understanding, this incomprehensible and all-glorious God will work in your heart and life and grant you in ever-growing measure to know Him in truth. "My eyes are upon You, O GOD the Lord; in You I take refuge" (Ps. 141:8). "Be still, and know that I am God" (46:10).

The Holiness of God (O.T.)

"Be holy, for I am holy. . . . For I the Lord sanctify them."
Leviticus 11:45; 21:23

NINE times these phrases are repeated in Leviticus. Israel had to learn that as holiness is the highest and most glorious attribute of God, so it must be the marked characteristic of His people. Those who want to know God properly, and meet with Him in the secret place, must above all desire to be holy as He is holy. The priests who were to have access to God had to be set apart for a life of holiness.

It was the same for the prophets who spoke for Him. Isaiah said, "I saw the Lord sitting on a throne, high and lifted up. . . . And one [seraph] cried to another and said: 'Holy, holy, holy is the Lord of hosts'" (6:1–3). This is the voice of adoration. "Then I said: 'Woe is me, for I am undone! . . . For my eyes have seen the King, the Lord of hosts'" (6:5). This is the voice of a broken, contrite heart. "Then one of the seraphim flew to me, having in his hand a live coal . . . from the altar. And he touched my mouth with it, and said: 'Behold . . . your iniquity is taken away, and your sin purged'" (6:6–7). This is the voice of grace and full redemption.

Then follows the voice of God: "Whom shall I send?" And the willing answer is, "Here am I! Send me" (6:8). Pause with holy fear and ask God to reveal Himself as the Holy One. "For thus says the High and Lofty One who inhabits eternity, whose name is Holy: 'I dwell in the high and holy place, with him who has a contrite and humble spirit'" (Isa. 57:15).

Be still, and take time to worship God in His great glory, and in His deep humility in which He longs and offers to dwell with us and in us. If you want to meet with your Father in the secret place, bow low and worship Him in the glory of His holiness. Give Him time to make Himself known to you. It is an unspeakable grace to know God as the Holy One. "You shall be holy, for I the LORD your God am holy" (Lev. 19:2); "Holy, holy, holy is the LORD of hosts" (Isa. 6:3); "Oh, worship the LORD in the beauty of holiness!" (Ps. 96:9); "And let the beauty of the LORD our God be upon us" (90:17).

The Holiness of God (N.T.)

"Holy Father, keep through Your name those whom You have given Me. . . . Sanctify them by Your truth. . . . And for their sakes I sanctify Myself, that they also may be sanctified by the truth."

John 17:11, 17, 19

CHRIST forever lives to pray this great prayer. Expect and appropriate God's answer. Hear the words of Paul in First Thessalonians: "Night and day praying exceedingly . . . that He may establish your hearts blameless in holiness before our God. . . . Now may the God of peace Himself sanctify you completely. . . . He who calls you is faithful, who also will do it" (3:10, 13; 5:23–24).

Ponder deeply these words as you read them, and use them as a prayer to God: "Blessed Lord, strengthen my heart to be blameless in holiness. May God Himself sanctify me completely. I know God is faithful, who also will do it."

What a privilege to commune with God in secret, to speak these words in prayer, and to wait on Him until they live in our hearts through the working of the Spirit and we begin to know something of the holiness of God. "To the church of God which is at Corinth, to those who are sanctified in Christ Jesus, called to be saints" (1 Cor. 1:2). This is God's calling for you and me.

God's holiness has been clearly revealed in the Old Testament. In the New, we find the holiness of God's people in Christ, through the sanctification of the Spirit. May we understand the blessedness of saying, "Be holy, for I am holy" (Lev. 11:45). God is saying, "With you, O My children, as with Me, holiness should be the chief thing."

For this purpose the Holy, Holy, Holy One has revealed Himself to us, through the Son and the Holy Spirit. Let us use the word "holy" with great reverence of God, and then with holy desire for ourselves. Worship the God who says, "I am the Lord who sanctifies you" (22:32). Bow before Him in holy fear and strong desire, and then, in the fullness of faith, listen to this prayer promise: "Now may the God of peace Himself sanctify you completely . . . who also will do it."

Sin

And the grace of our Lord was exceedingly abundant, with faith and love which are in Christ Jesus . . . to save sinners, of whom I am chief.

1 Timothy 1:14–15

NEVER forget for a moment, as you enter the secret place of prayer, that your whole relationship to God depends on what you think about sin and about yourself as a redeemed sinner. It is sin that makes God's holiness so glorious, because He has said, "Be holy, for . . . I am the LORD who sanctifies you" (Lev. 20:7–8).

It is sin that called forth the wonderful love of God in not sparing His Son. It was sin that nailed Jesus to the cross, and revealed the depth and the power of the love with which He loved. Through all eternity in the glory of heaven, it is our being redeemed sinners that will tune our praise.

Never for a moment forget that it is sin that has led to the great transaction between you and Christ Jesus; and that each day in your fellowship with God, His one aim is to deliver and keep you fully from its power and lift you up into His likeness and His infinite love.

It is the awareness of sin that will keep you low at His feet and give a deep undertone to all your adoration. It is the awareness of sin, always surrounding you and seeking to tempt you, that will give fervency to your prayers and urgency to the faith that hides itself in Christ. It is the awareness of sin that makes Christ so unspeakably precious, that keeps you every moment dependent on His grace, and gives you the ability to be more than a conqueror through Him who loved us. It is the awareness of sin that calls us to thank God with a broken and contrite heart which God will not despise, that works in us that contrite and humble spirit in which He delights to dwell.

It is in the inner chamber, in the secret place with the Father, that sin can be conquered, the holiness of Christ can be imparted, and the Spirit of holiness can take possession of our lives. In the inner chamber we learn to know and experience fully the divine power of these precious words of promise: "The blood of Jesus Christ His Son cleanses us from all sin. . . . Whoever abides in Him does not sin" (1 John 1:7; 3:6).

The Mercy of God

Oh, give thanks to the Lord, for He is good! For His mercy endures forever.

Psalm 136:1

THIS psalm is wholly devoted to the praise of God's mercy. In each of the twenty-six verses we have the expression, "His mercy endures forever." The psalmist was full of this happy thought. Our hearts too should be filled with this blessed assurance. The everlasting, unchangeable mercy of God is cause for unceasing praise and thanksgiving!

Let us read now what is said about God's mercy in the well-known Psalm 103: "Bless the Lord, O my soul . . . who crowns you with lovingkindness and tender mercies" (103:1, 4). Of all God's communicable attributes, mercy is the crown. May it be a crown upon my head and in my life! "The Lord is merciful and gracious, slow to anger, and abounding in mercy" (103:8).

Just as God's greatness is wonderful, so His mercy is infinite. "For as the heavens are high above the earth, so great is His mercy toward those who fear Him" (103:11). What a thought! As high as the heaven is above the earth, so immeasurably and inconceivably great is the mercy of God, waiting to bestow His richest blessing. "The mercy of the Lord is from everlasting to everlasting on those who fear Him" (103:17). Here again the psalmist speaks of God's boundless lovingkindness and mercy.

How frequently we read these familiar words without the least thought of their immeasurable greatness! Be still and meditate, until your heart responds as in the words of Psalm 36: "Your mercy, O LORD, is in the heavens" (36:5). "How precious is Your lovingkindness, O God! Therefore the children of men put their trust under the shadow of Your wings" (36:7). "Oh, continue Your lovingkindness to those who know You" (36:10).

Take time to thank God with great joy for the wonderful mercy with which He crowns your life, and say, "Your lovingkindness is better than life" (63:3).

The Word of God

For the Word of God is living and powerful.

Hebrews 4:12

TO have communion with God, His Word and prayer are both indispensable; and in the inner chamber they should not be separated. In His Word, God speaks to me; in prayer, I speak to God.

The Word teaches me also to know the God to whom I pray; it teaches me how He wants me to pray. It gives me precious promises to encourage me in prayer. It often gives me wonderful answers to prayer. The Word comes from God's heart and brings His thoughts and His love into my heart. And then the Word goes back from my heart into His great heart of love, and prayer is the means of fellowship between God's heart and mine.

The Word teaches me God's will—the will of His promises as to what He will do for me (as food for my faith), and also the will of His commands, to which I surrender myself in loving obedience.

The more I pray, the more I feel my need of the Word and rejoice in it. The more I read God's Word, the more I have to pray about and the more power I have in prayer. One great cause of prayerlessness is that we read God's Word too little, or only superficially, or in the light of human wisdom.

It is the Holy Spirit through whom the Word has been spoken; He is also the Spirit of prayer. He will teach me how to receive the Word and how to approach God. How blessed would the inner chamber be—what a power and an inspiration in our worship—if we only took God's Word as from Himself, turning it into prayer and definitely expecting an answer. In the inner chamber, in the secret of God's presence, God's Word becomes, through the Holy Spirit, our delight and our strength. God's Word—in deepest reverence in our hearts, on our lips, and in our lives—will be a never-failing fountain of strength and blessing.

Let us believe that God's Word is truly full of a quickening power to make us strong, enabling us to expect and receive great things from God. Above all, it gives us daily blessed fellowship with Him as the living God. "Blessed is the man . . . [whose] delight is in the law of the LORD, and in His law he meditates day and night" (Ps. 1:1–2).

The Psalms

How sweet are Your words to my taste! Sweeter than honey to my mouth!

Psalm 119:103

OF the sixty-six books in the Bible, the Book of Psalms is given to us specifically to help us to worship God. The other books are historical, or doctrinal, or practical. But the psalms take us into the inner sanctuary of God's holy presence to enjoy the blessedness of fellowship with Him. It is a book of devotions inspired by the Holy Spirit. Do you want to truly meet God each morning, and worship Him in spirit and in truth? Then let your heart be filled with the Word of God through these psalms.

As you read the Book of Psalms, underline the word "Lord" or "God" wherever it occurs, and also the pronouns referring to God: "I," "You," "He." This will help to connect the contents of the psalm with God, who is the object of all prayer.

When you have taken the trouble to mark the different names of God, you will find that more than one difficult psalm will have light shed upon it. These underlined words will make God the central thought and lead you to a new worship of Him. Take them on your lips and speak them out before Him. Your faith will be strengthened anew to realize how God is your strength and help in all circumstances of life.

Just as the Holy Spirit in ancient times used these psalms to teach God's people to pray, they can also teach us, by the power of that same Spirit, to abide continually in God's presence.

Take Psalm 119, for example. Every time that the word "God," "Lord," "You," or "Your" occurs, underline it. You will be surprised to find that each verse contains these words once or more than once. Meditate on the thought that the God who is found throughout this whole psalm is the same God who gives us His law and will enable us to keep it. This psalm will soon become one of your most beloved, and you will find its prayers and its teaching concerning God's Word drawing you continually up to God, in the blessed consciousness of His power and love. "Oh, how I love Your law! It is my meditation all the day" (119:97).

Day 27

The Glory of God

To Him be glory . . . to all generations.

Ephesians 3:21

GOD Himself must reveal His glory to us; then alone are we able to know and glorify Him properly.

There is no more wonderful image of the glory of God in nature than the starry heavens. Telescopes, which are continually being made more powerful, have long proclaimed the wonders of God's universe. And through photography, new wonders of that glory have been revealed. If a photographic plate is fixed below a telescope, it can reveal millions of stars which cannot be seen by the eye through the best telescope. Man must step to one side and allow the glory of the heavens to reveal itself; then the stars, at first wholly invisible, and at immense distances, will leave their image upon the plate.

This is a lesson for those who long to see the glory of God in His Word. Put aside your own efforts and thoughts. Let your heart be as a photographic plate that waits for God's glory to be revealed. The plate must be rightly prepared and clean; let your heart be prepared and purified by God's Spirit. "Blessed are the pure in heart, for they shall see God" (Matt. 5:8). The plate must be immovable; let your heart be still before God. The plate must be exposed sometimes for seven or eight hours to receive the full impression of the farthest stars; let your heart take time in silent waiting upon God, and He will reveal His glory. If you keep silent before God and give Him time, He will put thoughts into your heart that may be of unspeakable blessing to yourself and others. He will create within you desires and dispositions that will be like the rays of His glory shining in you.

Put this to the test this morning. Offer your spirit to Him in deep humility and have faith that God will reveal Himself in His holy love. His glory will descend upon you; you will feel the need to give Him adequate time to do His blessed work. "The LORD is in His holy temple. Let all the earth keep silence before Him" (Hab. 2:20). "My soul, wait silently for God alone, for my expectation is from Him" (Ps. 62:5). "God . . . has shone in our hearts to give the light of the knowledge of the glory of God in the face of Jesus Christ" (2 Cor. 4:6). "Be still, and know that I am God" (Ps. 46:10).

The Holy Trinity

Elect according to the foreknowledge of God the Father, in sanctification of the Spirit, for obedience and sprinkling of the blood of Jesus Christ.

1 Peter 1:2

HERE we have one of the texts in which the great truth of the blessed Trinity is seen to lie at the very root of our spiritual life. In our adoration of God the Father, we need sufficient time each day to worship Him in His glorious attributes. But we must remember that, in all our communion with God, the presence and the power of the Son and the Spirit are absolutely necessary.

What a field this opens for us in the inner chamber. We need to take time to realize how our communion with the Father is the result of the active and personal presence and working of the Lord Jesus. It takes time to become fully conscious of the need I have of Him in every time I approach God, the confidence I can have in the work that He is doing for me and in me, and how, in holy and intimate love, I may count on His presence and all-prevailing intercession. But to learn that lesson requires time—and that time will be most blessedly rewarded!

It is the same with the divine and almighty power of the Holy Spirit working in the depth of my heart—as the One who alone is able to reveal the Son within me. Through Him alone I have the power to know what and how to pray—especially how to plead the name of

Jesus—and to receive the assurance that my prayer has been accepted.

Have you ever felt that it was a joke to speak of spending five minutes alone with God—as if that was all the time needed to sense His glory? Doesn't the thought of true worship of God in Christ through the Holy Spirit make you feel more than ever that it takes time to enter into such a holy alliance with God? By spending time in the secret of God's presence, you receive grace to abide in Christ and be led by His Spirit all day long.

Pause and think on this passage: "Elect according to the foreknowledge of God the Father, in sanctification of the Spirit, for obedience and sprinkling of the blood of Jesus Christ" (1 Pet. 1:2). What food for thought—and worship! "When You said, 'Seek My face,' my heart said to You, 'Your face, Lord, I will seek'" (Ps. 27:8).

The Love of God

God is love, and he who abides in love abides in God, and God in him.

1 John 4:16

THE best and most wonderful word in heaven is love, for God is love. And the best and most wonderful word in the inner chamber of prayer must be love, for the God who meets us there is love.

What is love? It is the deep desire to give oneself for the beloved. Love finds its joy in imparting all that it has to make the loved one happy. And the heavenly Father, who offers to meet us in the inner chamber—let there be no doubt of this in our minds—has no other object than to fill our hearts with His love.

All the other attributes of God which have been mentioned find in this their highest glory. The true and full blessing of the inner chamber is nothing less than a life in the abundant love of God.

Because of this, our first and foremost thought in the inner chamber should be faith in the love of God. As you pray, seek to exercise great and unbounded faith in the love of God. Take time in silence to meditate on the wonderful revelation of God's love in Christ until you are filled with the spirit of worship and wonder and longing desire. Take time to believe the precious truth that "the love of God has been poured out in our hearts by the Holy Spirit who was given to us" (Rom. 5:5).

We should be ashamed at how little we have believed in and sought after God's love. As we pray, we should be confident that our heavenly Father longs to manifest His love to us, and be deeply convinced of the truth that He will and can do it. "Yes, I have loved you with an everlasting love" (Jer. 31:3). "That you, being rooted and grounded in love, may be able to comprehend with all saints what is the width and length and depth and height—to know the love of Christ which passes knowledge" (Eph. 3:17–19). "Behold what manner of love the Father has bestowed on us" (1 John 3:1).

Waiting on God

On You I wait all the day.

Psalm 25:5

IN the expression "waiting on God" we find a deep scriptural truth about the attitude of the soul in communion with God. Just think—as we wait on God, He may reveal Himself in us; He may teach us His will; He may do to us what He has promised, that in all things He may be the Infinite God.

In this attitude of soul we should begin each day. On awaking in the morning, in prayer and meditation, in our daily work, in striving after obedience and holiness, in struggling against sin and self-will—in everything we should wait on God, to receive what He will bestow, to see what He will do, to allow Him to be Almighty God.

Meditate on these precious promises of God's Word, and discover the secret of heavenly power and joy: "But those who wait on the LORD shall renew their strength; they shall mount up with wings like eagles" (Isa. 40:31). "Wait on the LORD; be of good courage, and He shall strengthen your heart; wait, I say, on the LORD" (Ps. 27:14). "Rest in the LORD, and wait patiently for Him" (37:7).

The deep root of all scriptural theology is absolute dependence on God. As we practice this attitude, it will become more natural and blessedly possible to say, "On You I wait all the day." This is the secret of true, uninterrupted, silent adoration and worship. Have you begun to learn the true worship of God? If so, the Lord's name be praised. Or have you only learned how little you know of it? For this, too, thank Him. If you long for a fuller experience of this blessing, seek Him for it, recognizing your absolute need, each day and all the day, to wait on God. May the God of all grace grant this. "I wait for the LORD, my soul waits, and in His word I do hope" (Ps. 130:5). "Rest in the LORD, and wait patiently for Him . . . and He shall give you the desires of your heart" (37:7, 4).

The Praise of God

For praise from the upright is beautiful.

Psalm 33:1

PRAISE is always a part of adoration. Adoration, when it has entered God's presence, always leads to the praise of His name. Praise should be part of the incense we bring before God in our quiet time.

When the children of Israel crossed the Red Sea and were delivered from the power of Egypt, the joy of their redemption burst forth into a song of praise: "Who is like You, O LORD, among the gods? Who is like You, glorious in holiness, fearful in praises, doing wonders?" (Exod. 15:11).

In the Psalms we see what a large place praise ought to have in the spiritual life. There are more than sixty psalms of praise, and they occur more frequently as the book draws to its close. See Psalms 95–101, 103–107, 111–118, 134–138, 144–150. The last five are all "Hallelujah" (meaning "Praise the Lord") psalms, with the word appearing at the beginning and the end. And the very last repeats "praise Him" twice in every verse, and ends, "Let everything that has breath praise the LORD" (Ps. 150:6)

Let us take time to study this until our whole heart and life becomes one continual song of praise. "I will bless the LORD at all times; His praise shall continually be in my mouth" (34:1). "Every day I will bless You" (145:2).

"I will sing praises to my God while I have my being" (Ps. 146:2). With the coming of Christ into the world there was a new outburst of praise in the song of the angels, the song of Mary, the song of Zacharias, and the song of Simeon. And then to find in the song of Moses and the Lamb the praise of God filling creation: "Great and marvelous are Your works, Lord God Almighty! . . . Who shall not fear You, O Lord, and glorify Your name? For You alone are holy" (Rev. 15:3–4). The final song of praise is in Revelation 19:1–6, with four shouts of "Alleluia" followed by "For the Lord God Omnipotent reigns."

May your inner chamber of prayer and your quiet time with God always lead your heart to unceasing praise.

PUBLICATIONS

Fort Washington, PA 19034

This book is published by CLC Publications, an outreach of CLC Ministries International. The purpose of CLC is to make evangelical Christian literature available to all nations so that people may come to faith and maturity in the Lord Jesus Christ. We hope this book has been life changing and has enriched your walk with God through the work of the Holy Spirit. If you would like to know more about CLC, we invite you to visit our website:

www.clcusa.org

To know more about the remarkable story of the founding of CLC International we encourage you to read

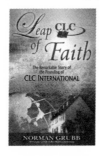

LEAP OF FAITH

Norman Grubb

Paperback
Size 5¼ x 8, Pages 248
ISBN: 978-0-87508-650-7
ISBN (e-book): 978-1-61958-055-8

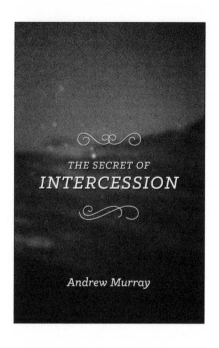

THE SECRET OF INTERCESSION

Andrew Murray

The Secret Series books contain a wealth of teaching that is based on Andrew Murray's mature and full experience in Christ. *The Secret of Intercession* contains one month of daily selections that reveal the power of intercession.

Paperback
Size 4¹/₄ x 7, Pages 67
ISBN: 978-1-61958-249-1
ISBN (*e-book*): 978-1-61958-250-7

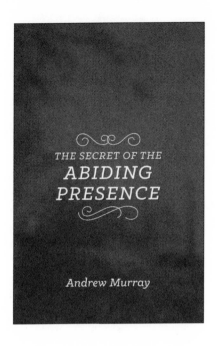

THE SECRET OF THE ABIDING PRESENCE

Andrew Murray

The Secret Series books contain a wealth of teaching that is based on Andrew Murray's mature and full experience in Christ. *The Secret of the Abiding Presence* contains one month of daily selections that reveal the peace that comes with resting in the presence of God.

Paperback
Size 4¹/₄ x 7, Pages 67
ISBN: 978-1-61958-251-4
ISBN (*e-book*): 978-1-61958-252-1

ANDREW MURRAY:
THE AUTHORIZED BIOGRAPHY

Leona Choy

A nineteenth-century missionary statesman, revivalist, evangelist, and pastor, Andrew Murray is one of the best-loved and most widely read writers on the deeper life. Many of today's readers, however, are unaware of the struggles and steps of faith which molded this servant of God into an exceptional teacher of faith, prayer, and Spirit-filled living.

Paperback
Size 5¼ x 8½, Pages 267
ISBN: 978-0-87508-829-7
ISBN (*e-book*): 978-1-61958-105-0